Meteors

By Heather Hammonds

Illustrations by Chantal Stewart

Contents

Shooting Stars

Troy was staying at Jason's house on Saturday night. They were watching their favourite movie when Jason's mum came into the room.

"Turn off all the lights," said Mum, "and come outside. Something special is happening tonight."

Jason and Troy weren't happy. They were in the middle of watching a really exciting movie and it was cold and dark outside. They reluctantly followed Jason's mum into the garden.

"Look up at the sky, boys," said Mum.

"What are we looking for?" asked Troy. "Aliens?"

"No," laughed Jason's mum. "Just keep looking up. You might see something amazing."

Suddenly, a bright orange light raced across the sky. "Wow! It's an alien!" yelled Jason.

"No, it's not," laughed Troy. "It's a shooting star. Look! There are lots of them."

"This is amazing!" shouted Jason. "Quick, Troy! You count them and I'll make a chart showing the colour and the time they appear."

"Shooting stars are really meteors," explained Jason's mum. "They are little pieces of dust and rock from space that fall towards Earth and burn up in the sky."

"Watching shooting stars is much better than watching movie stars on TV," said Jason.

Time	Meteors seen	Colour
8.00	2	White
8.03	1	Orange
8.09	3	White
8.12	2	White
8.15	2	Orange

How Meteors Are Formed

Meteors begin as small pieces of dust or rock, called meteoroids. Meteoroids often come from the tail of a comet.

When a comet passes the Sun, the heat from the Sun can cause parts of the comet to melt. Pieces of rock, or meteoroids, are left behind in space as the comet travels on.

As the Earth travels around the Sun, it passes through the paths of many meteoroids.

Some of these meteoroids enter the Earth's atmosphere and fall towards the Earth.

Meteoroids that enter the Earth's atmosphere are called meteors.

As the meteoroids travel through the Earth's atmosphere, they become very hot. They become so hot that they begin to burn up and glow brightly.

If a large number of meteoroids enter the Earth's atmosphere at the same time, the bright glow looks like a shower of shooting stars.

Meteors are what we see in the sky when meteoroids in space heat up and glow as they fall towards the Earth.